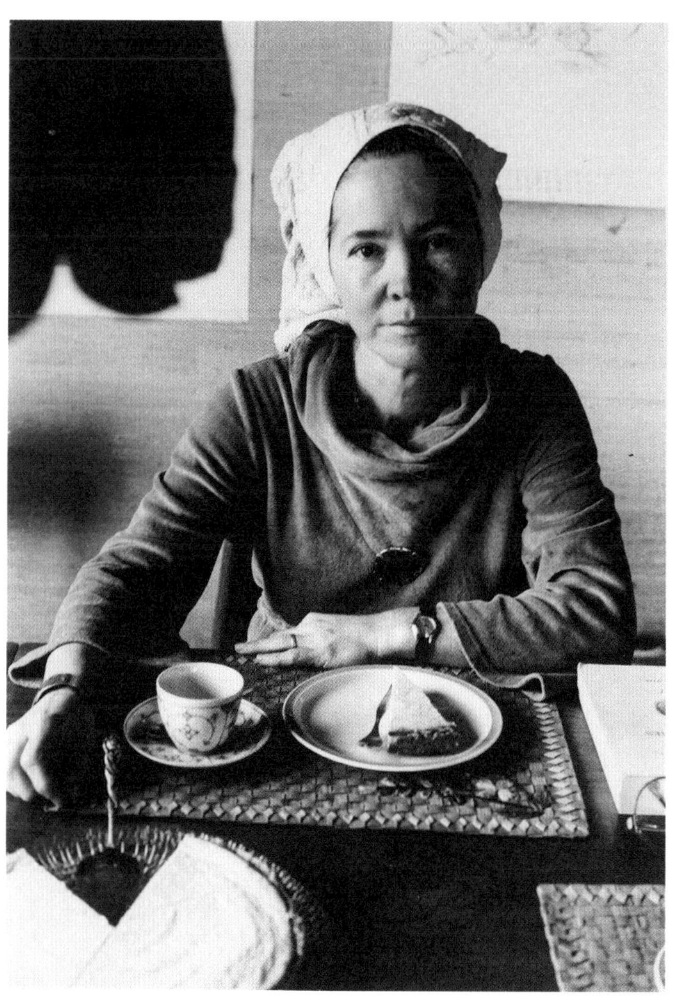

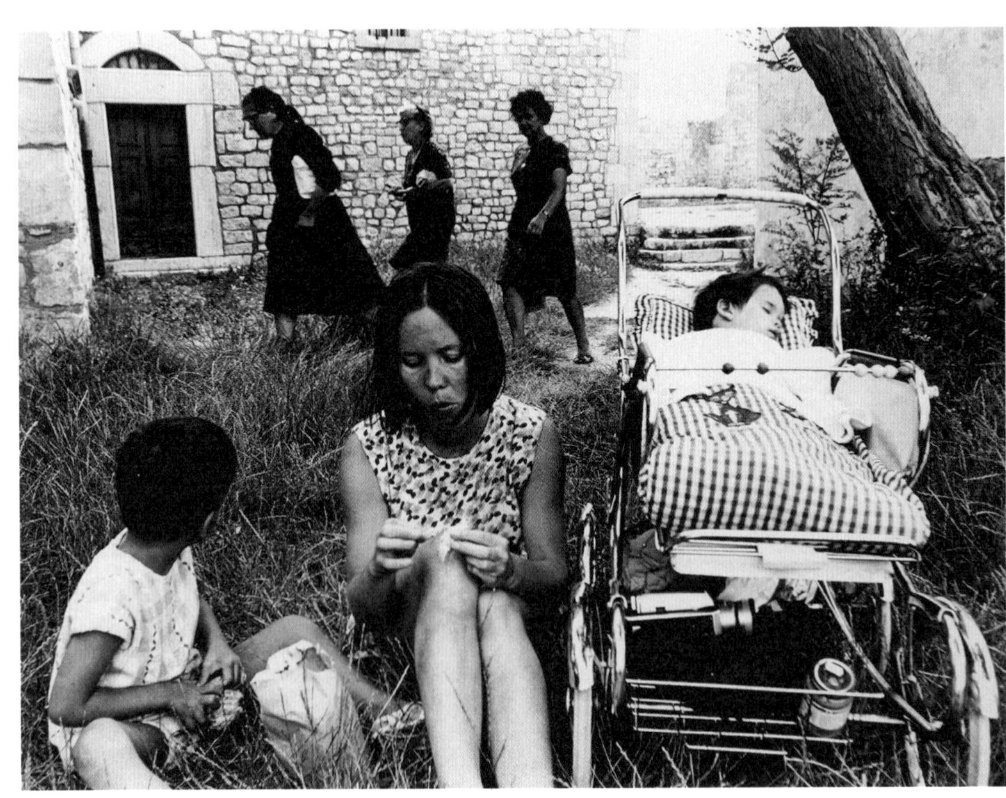

Just Life

The camera was a constant companion in the life of the engineer Peter Dammann (born in 1936). Employed in airplane development at Lake Constance in southern Germany, he was encouraged by a friend at work to purchase his first camera, a Praktina IIa from Dresden. Between the 1960s and 1990s he not only photographed his family, but also people, situations, landscapes, and animals. He produced thousands of images of family celebrations, excursions, birthdays, and funerals. In this way he created a family history of the sort that will be familiar to many. Yet he was more interested in creating good images than in mere documentation. Like many other amateur photographers Dammann looked to established, known photographers and trained his eye with their pictures. His first analog camera was followed by many other models, thus documenting his fascination for precision mechanics and optics as an engineer.

Dammann preferred black-and-white photography, and he made his own prints. In his different apartments over the years he had a darkroom in the bathroom, in a storage room, and later in a basement room. He collected everything in orderly, labeled binders, boxes, and crates, carefully organized in plastic sleeves and stored together with the corresponding contact sheets. Those photographs that Dammann considered the best were enlarged to a format of 18 by 24 centimeters, which he stored in homemade wooden crates. The last roll of black-and-white film that he developed bears the number 422 and is from the year 2007. He digitized the last eighty-nine rolls of black-and-white film himself and then ordered prints from a photo service. Since 2002 his photography and archives are digital.

In spite of his ambitions as a designer, Peter Dammann never intended to exhibit his personal family chronicle. His son, the artist Martin Dammann (born in 1965), encouraged his father to publically show his private photographs for the first time in this publication and in the exhibition at the Opelvillen.

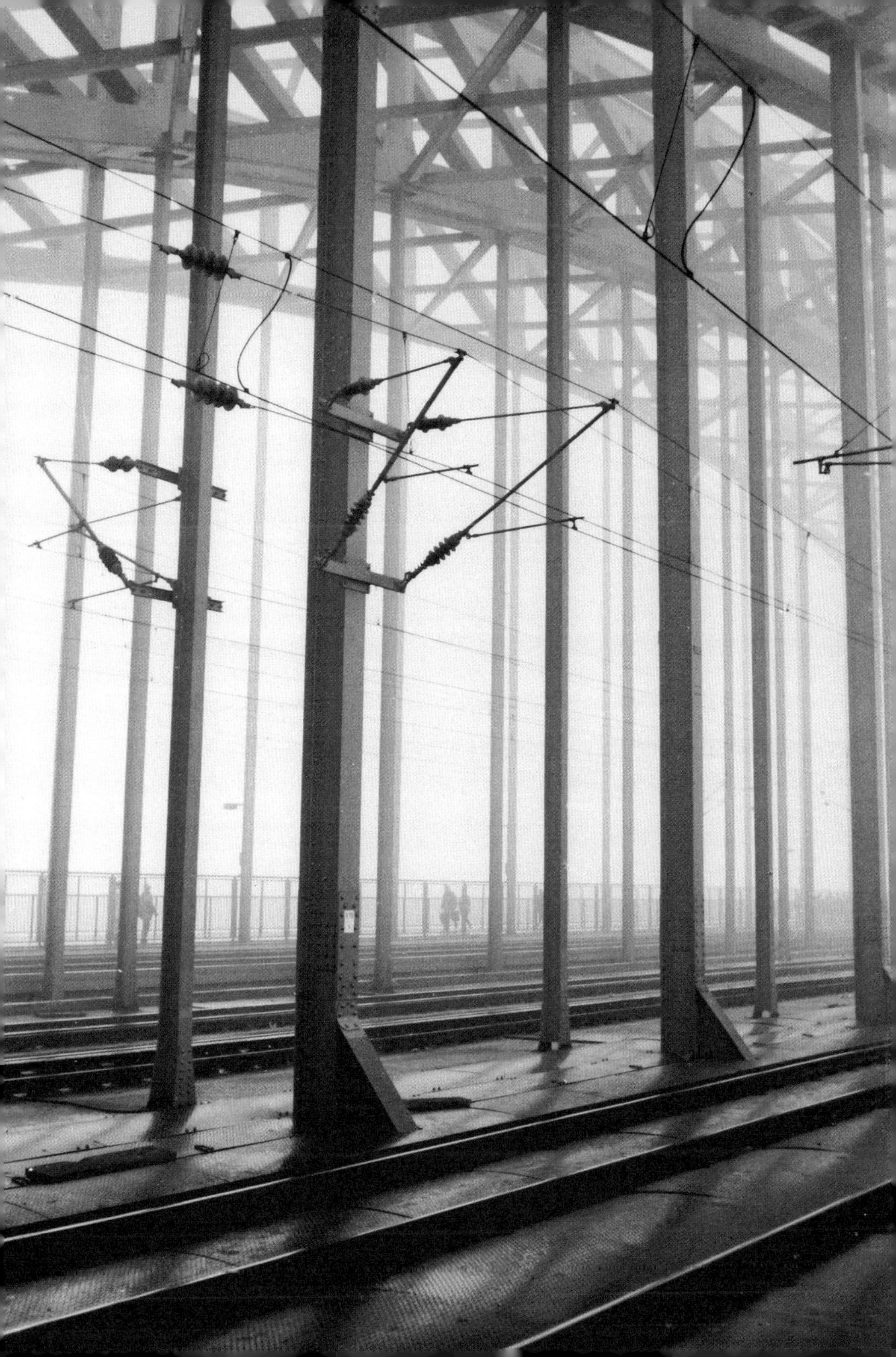

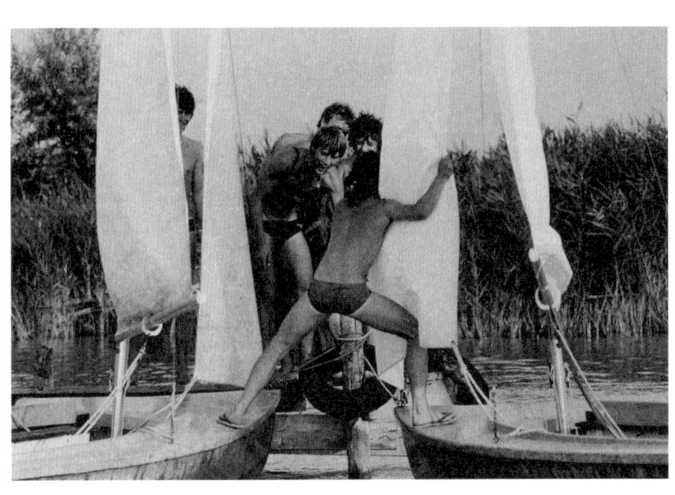

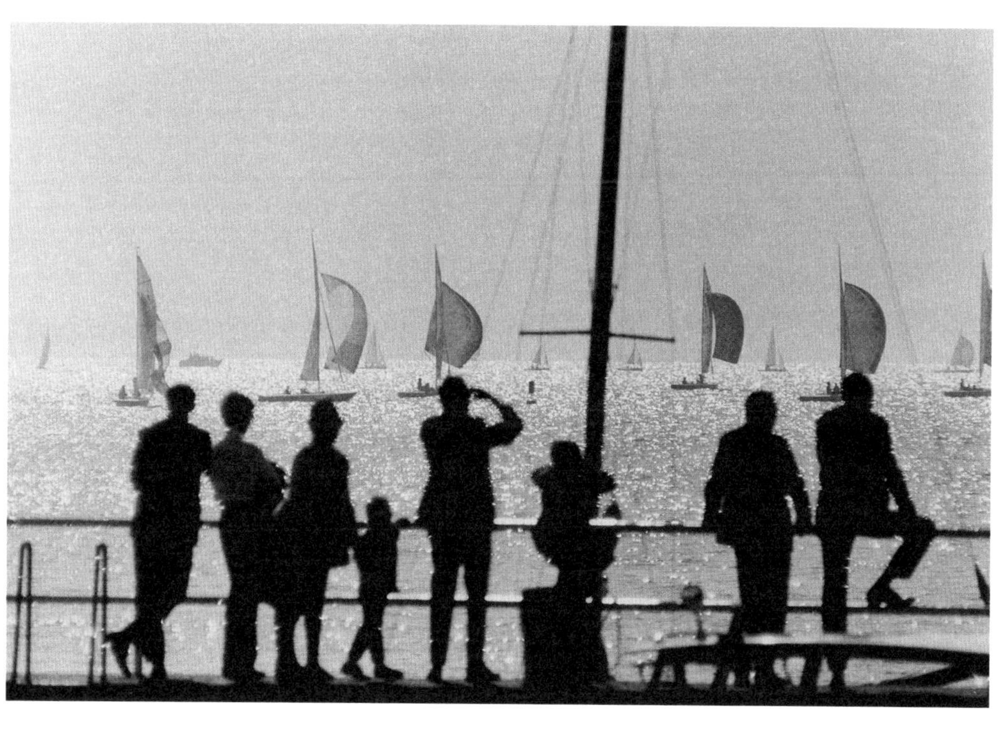

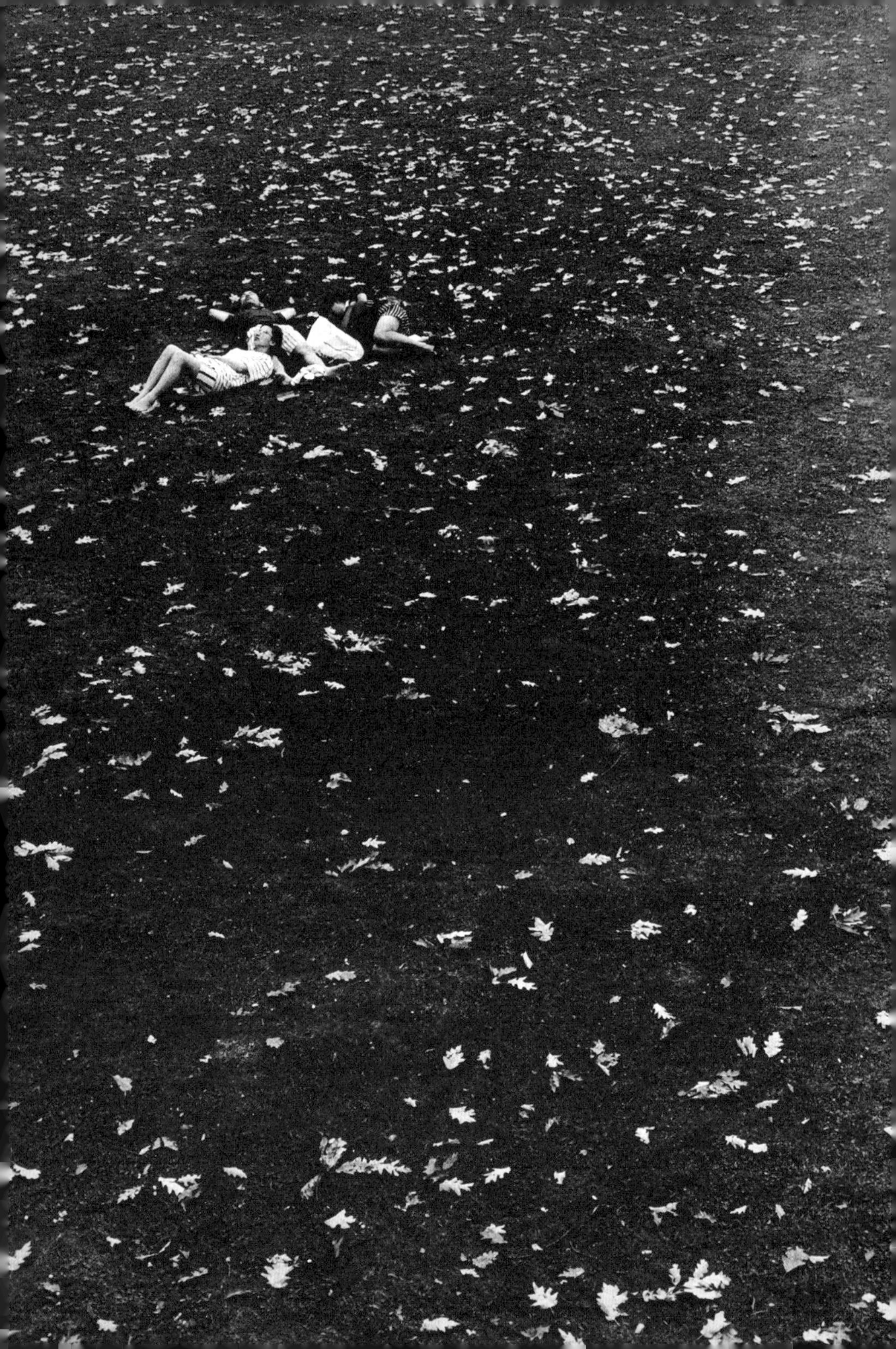

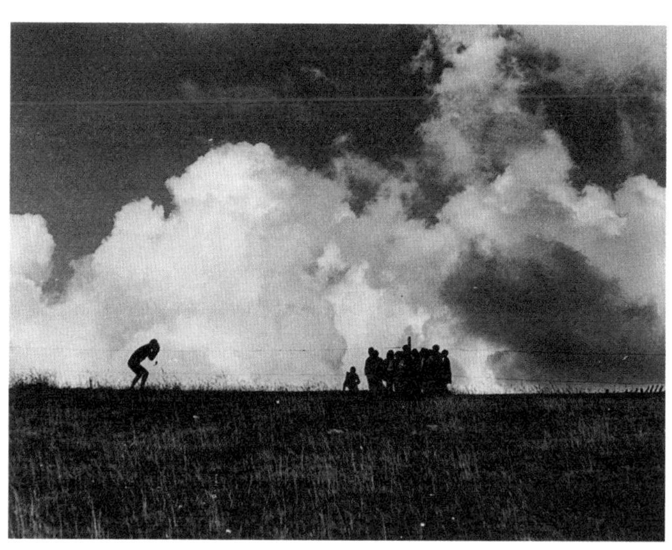

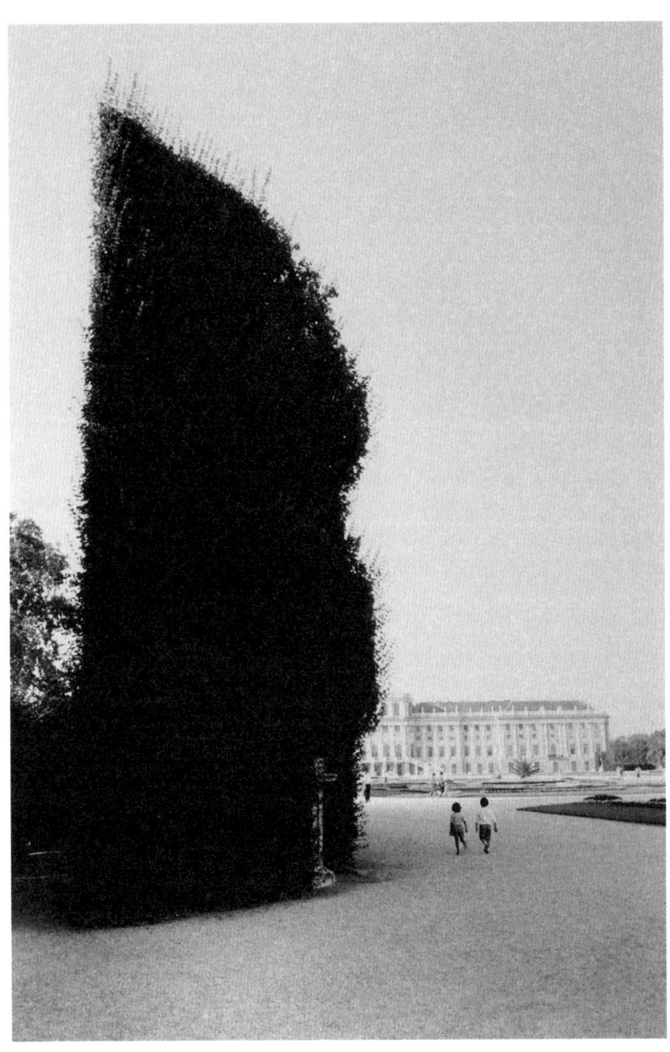

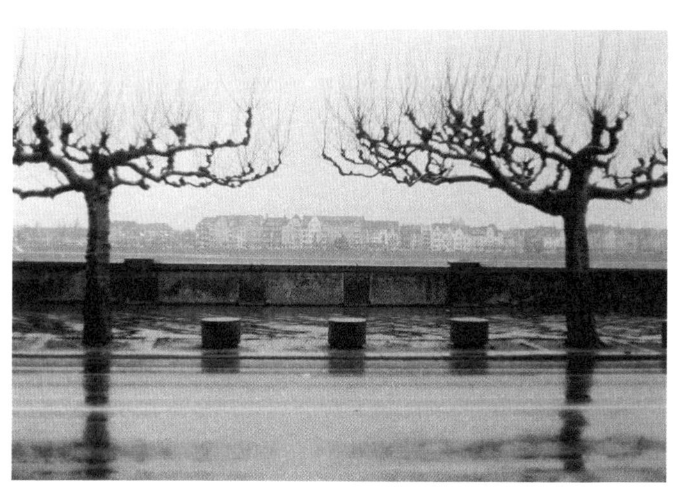

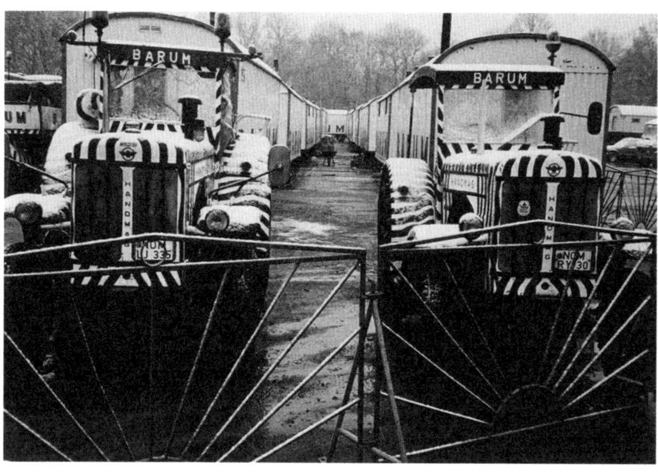
BARUM
BARUM

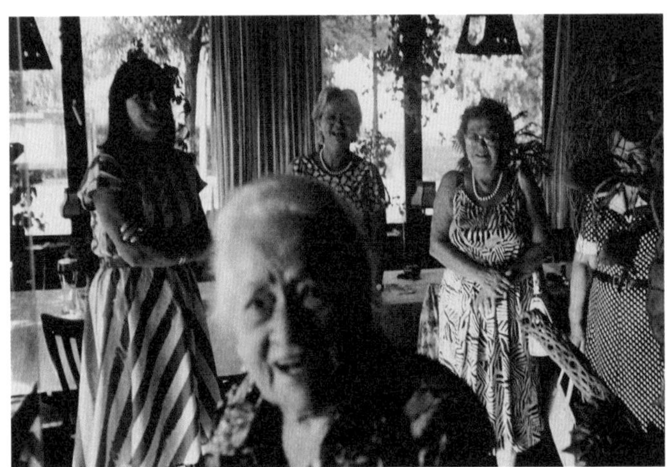

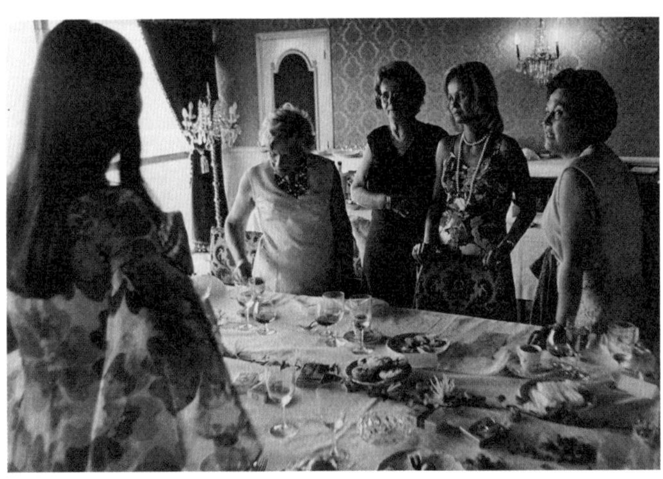

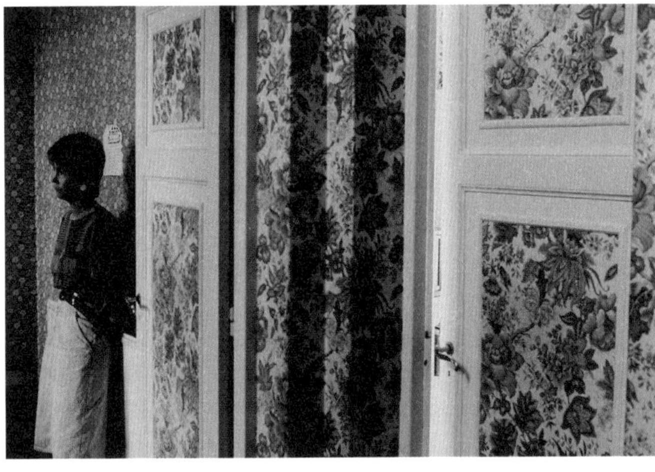

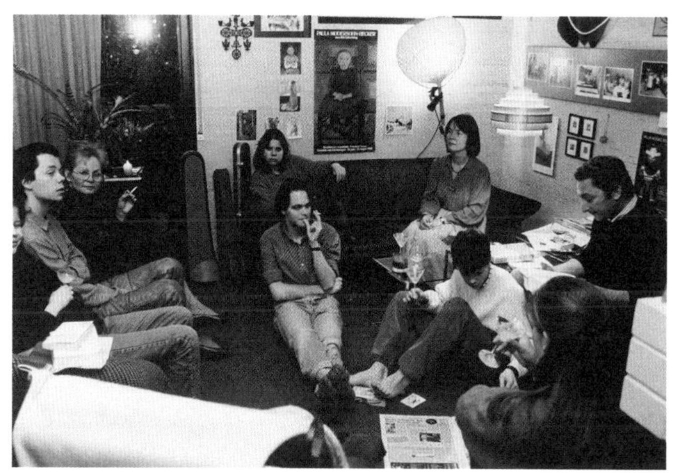

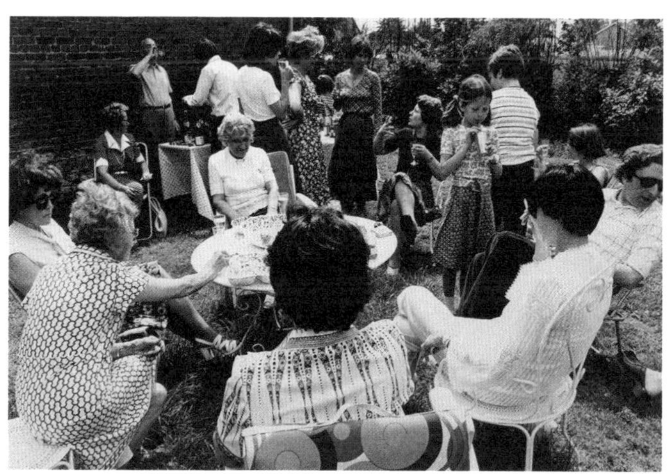

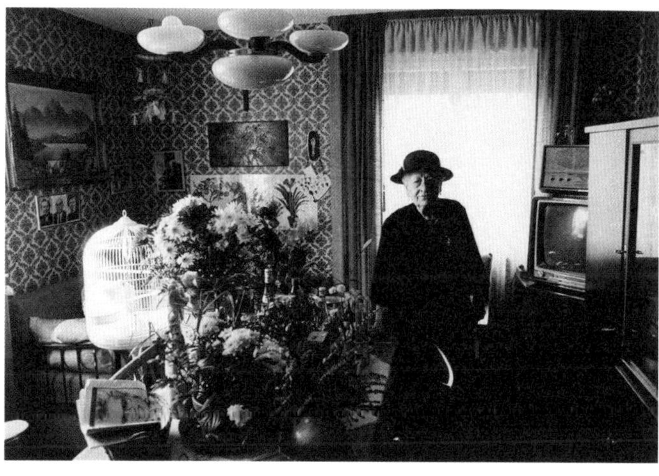

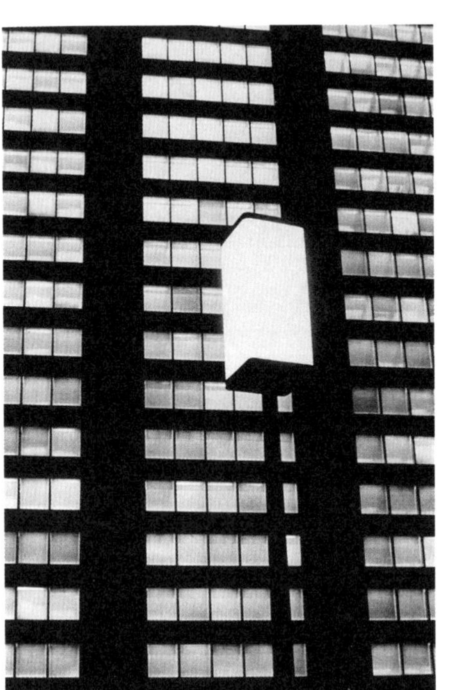

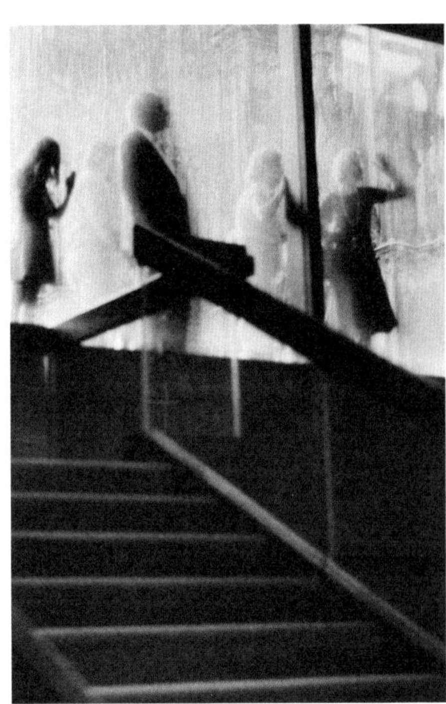

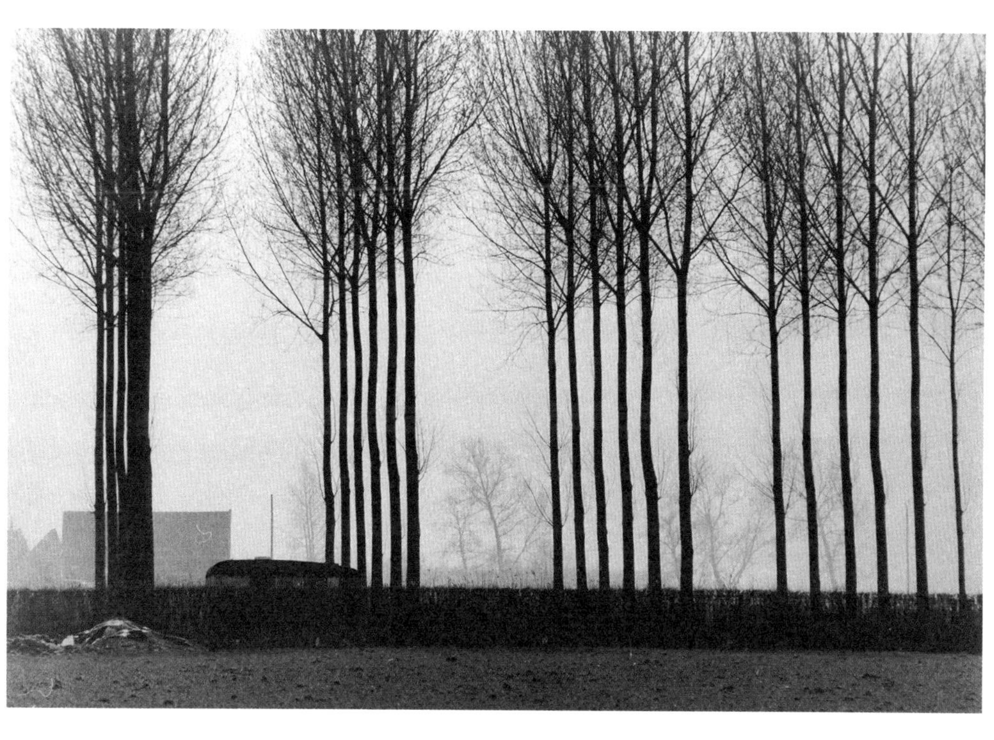

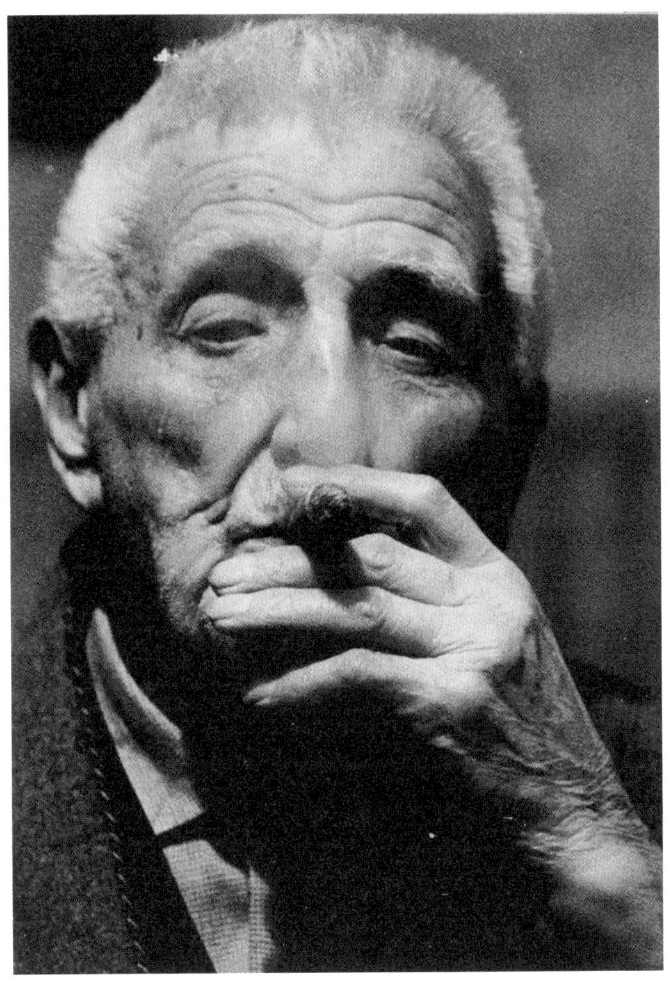

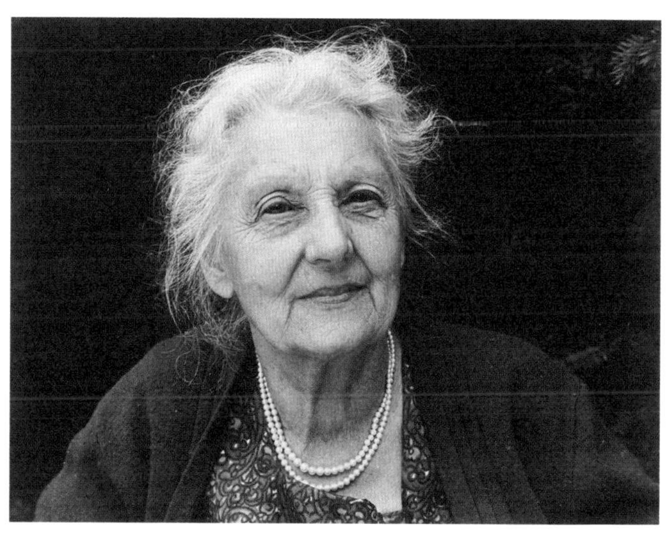

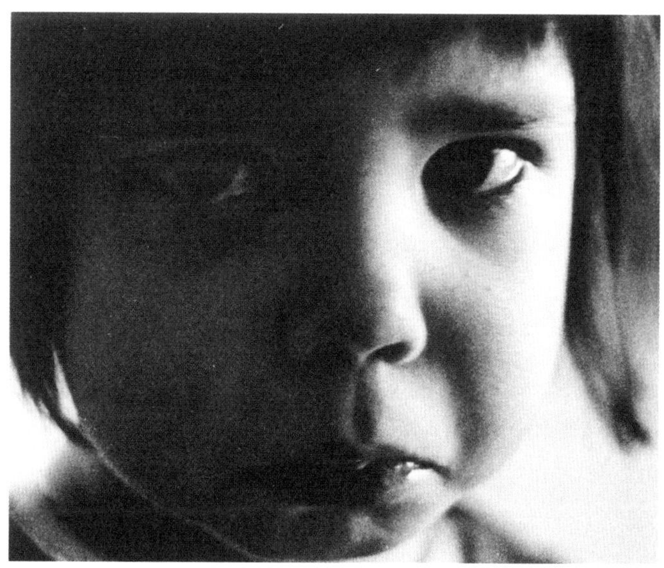

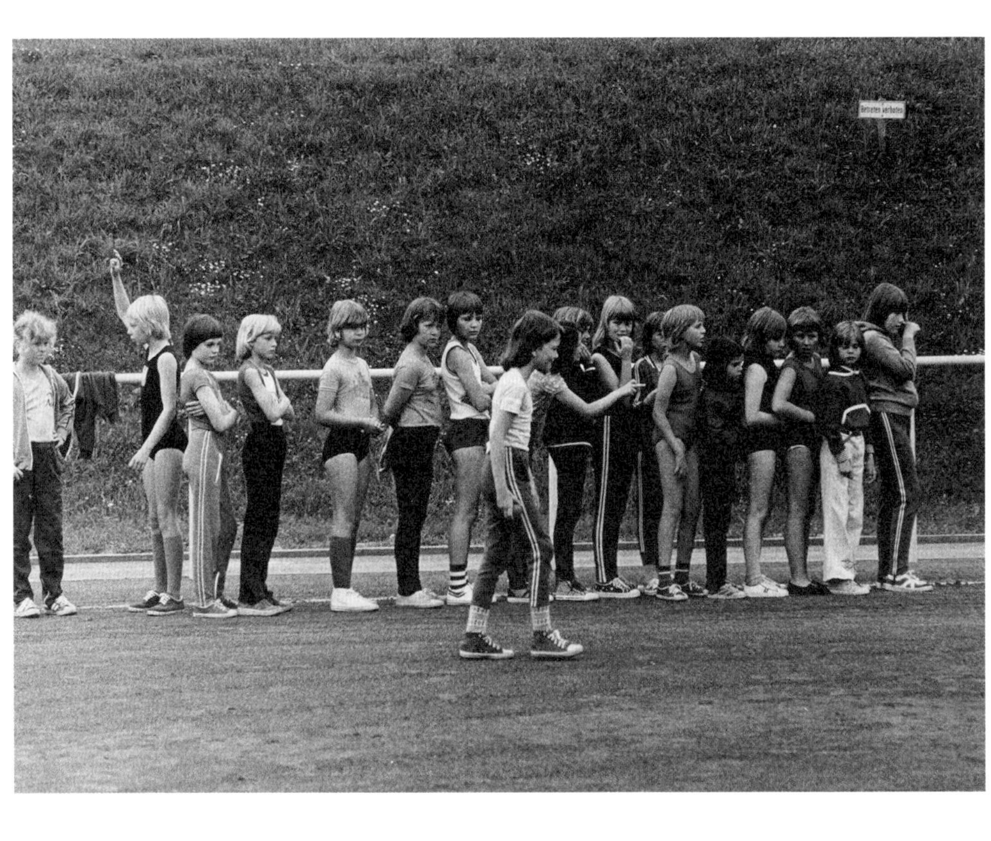
Betreten verboten

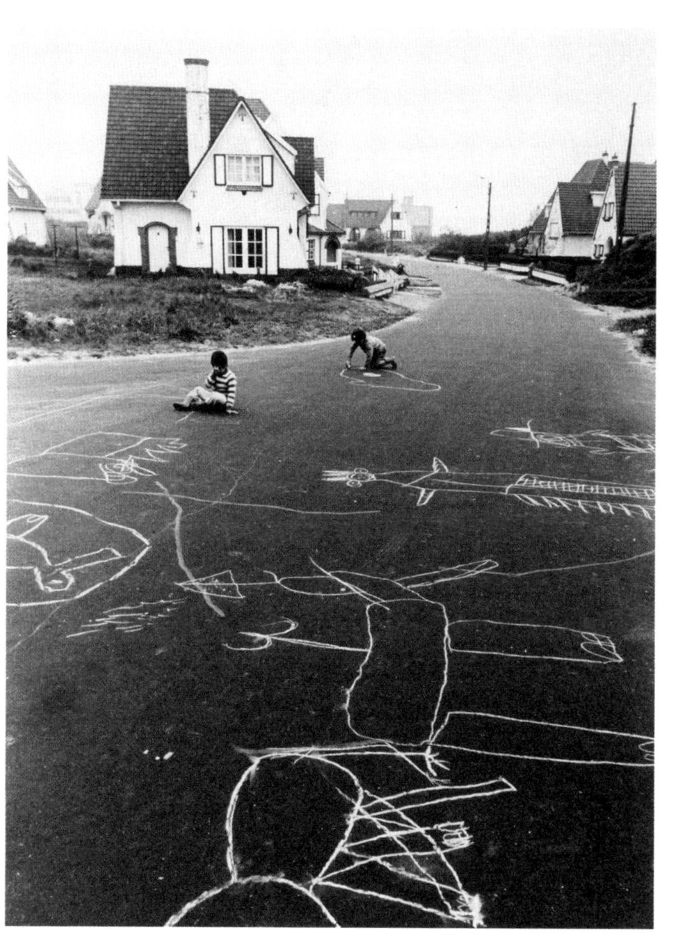

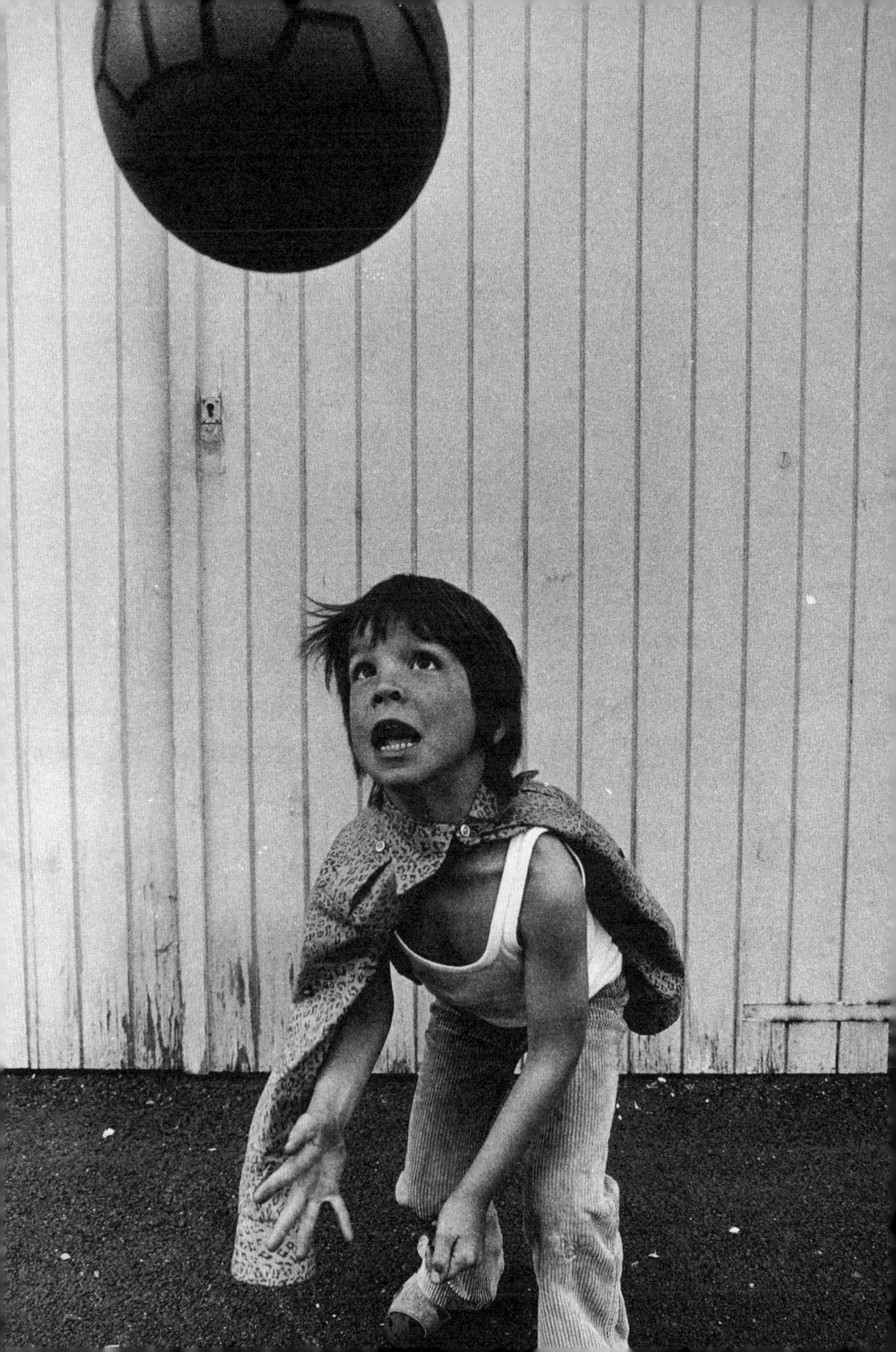

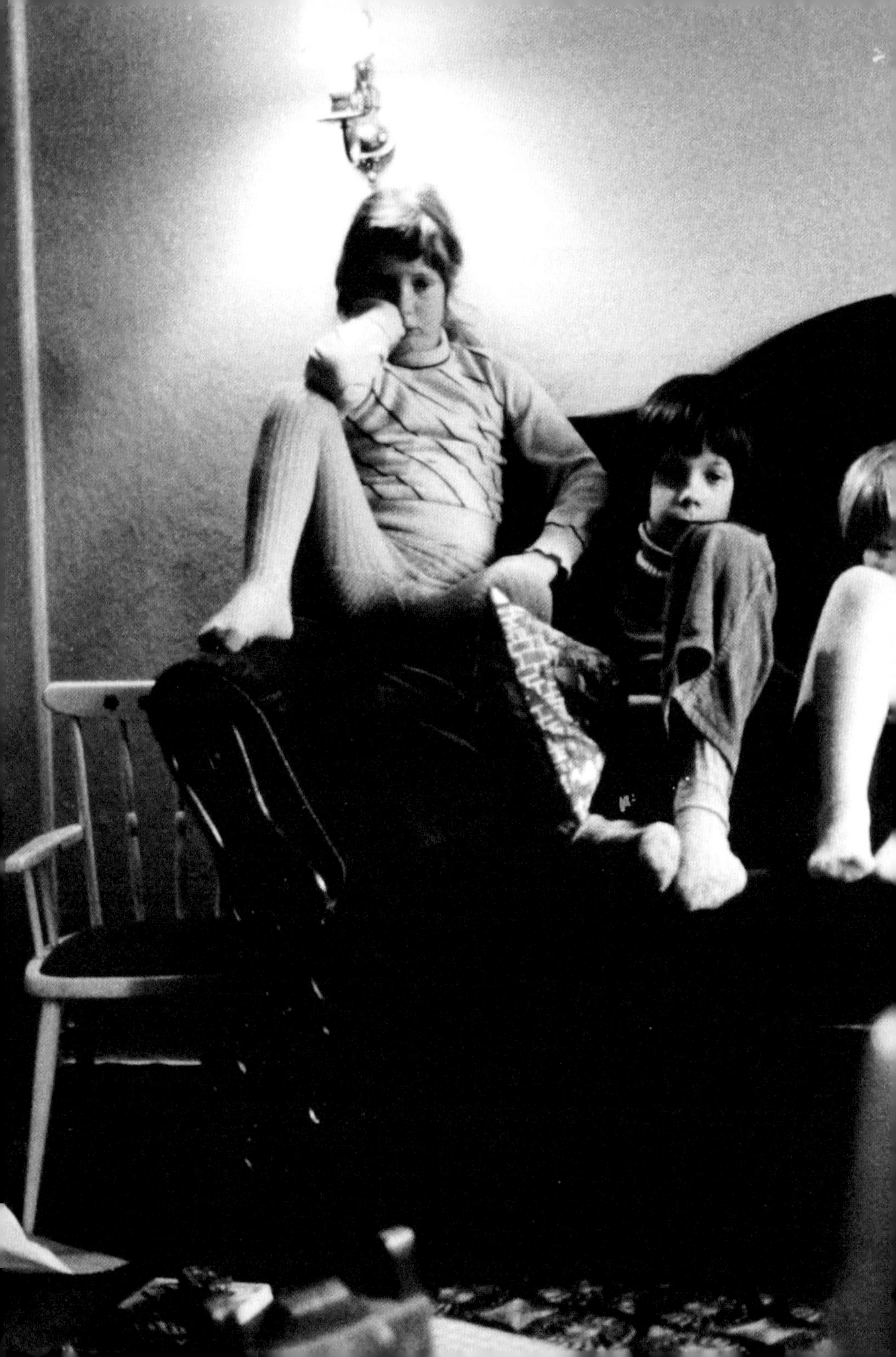

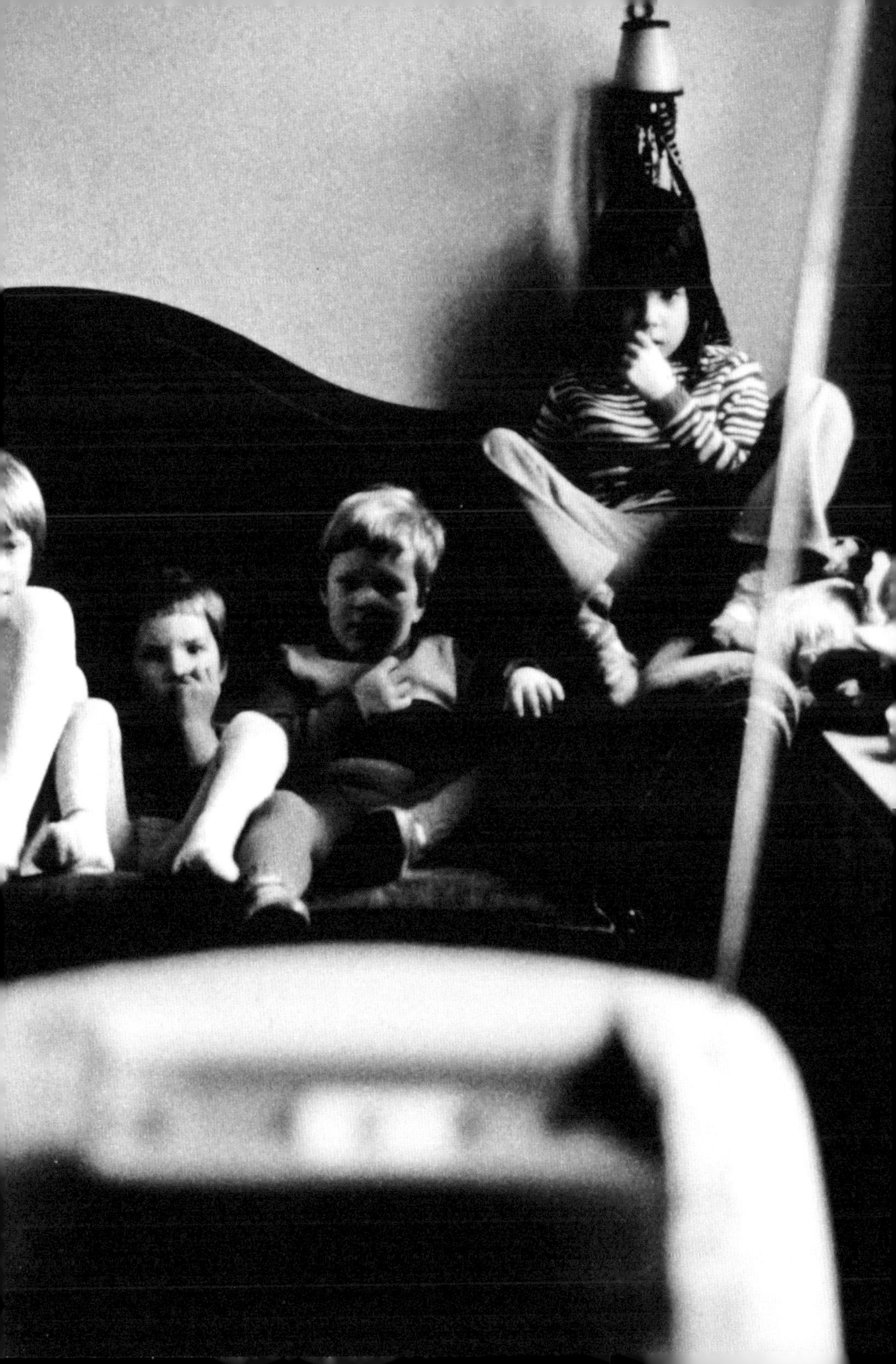

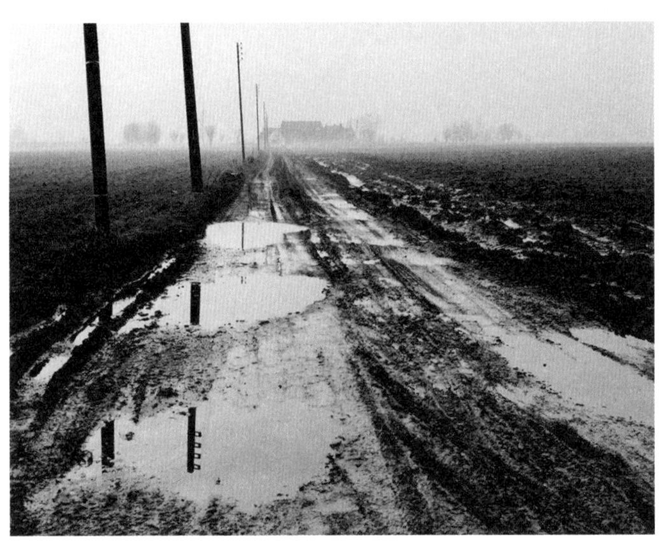

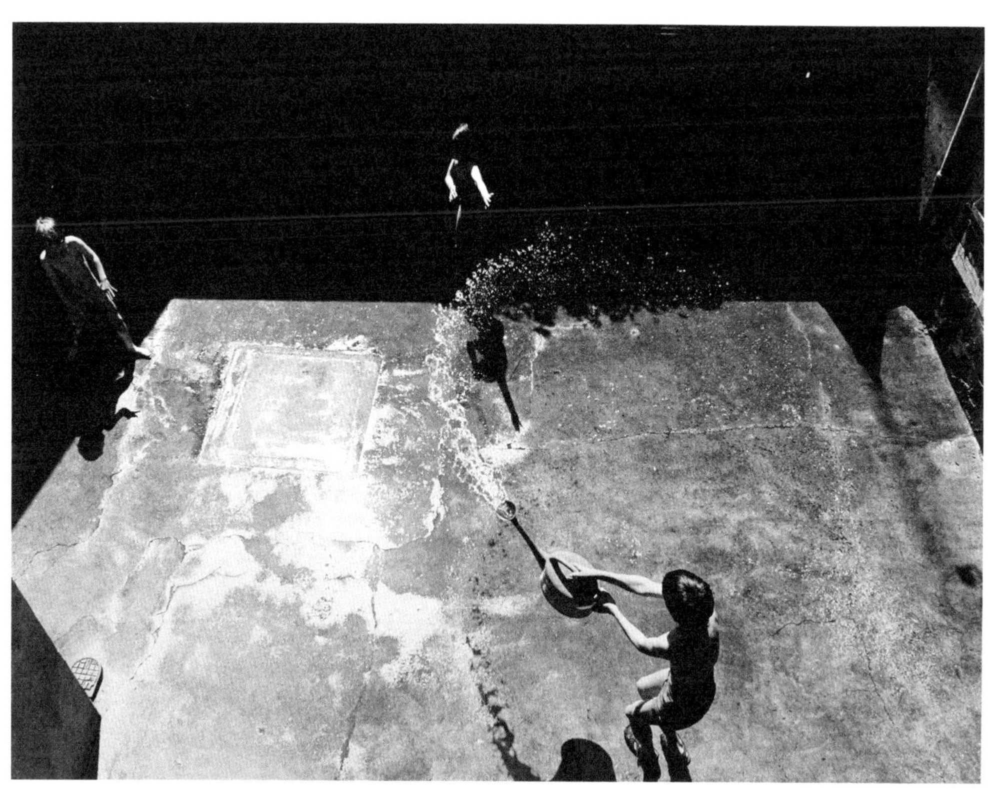

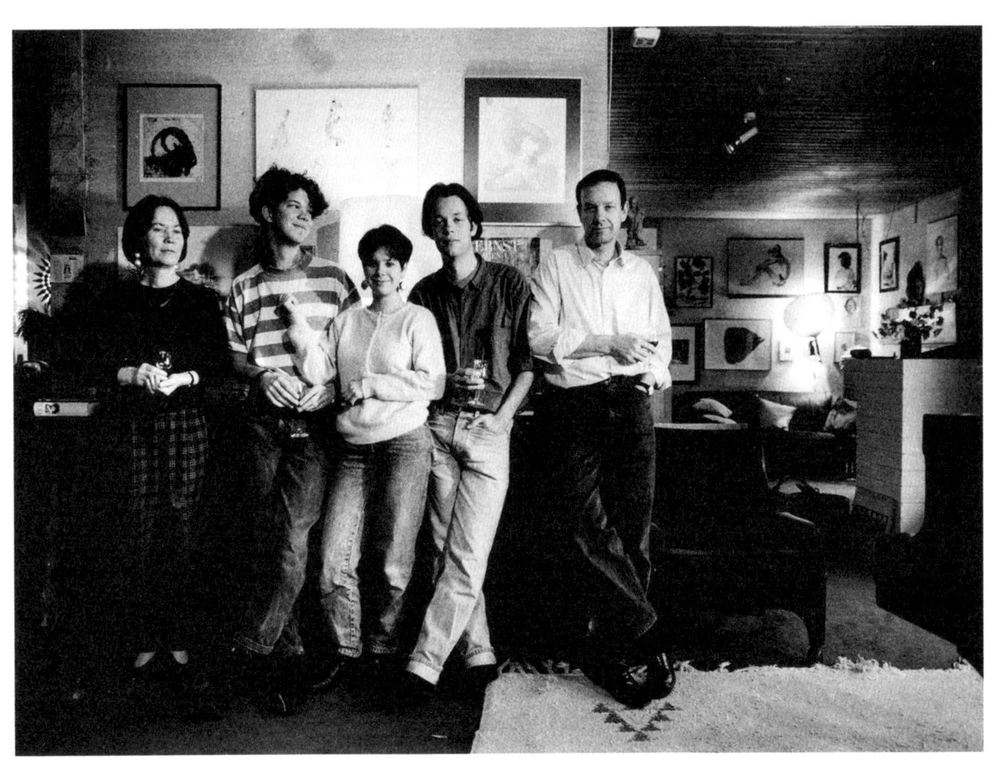

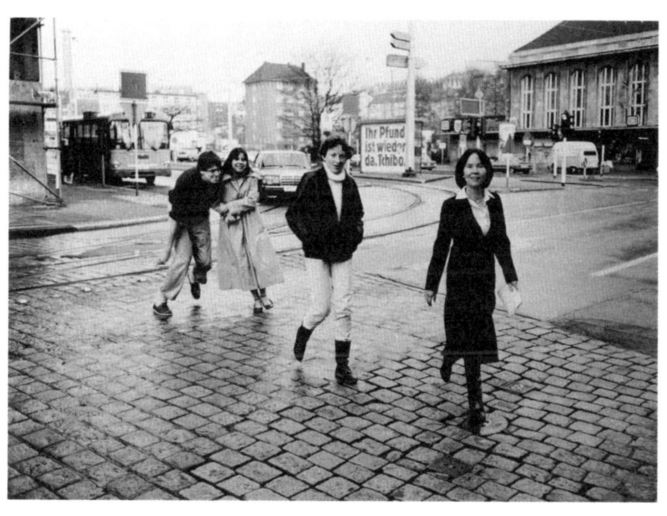
Ihr Pfund
ist wieder
da. Tchibo

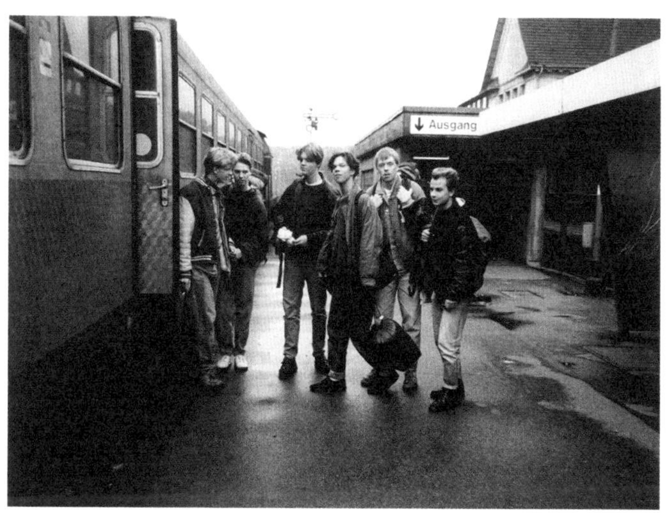
Ausgang

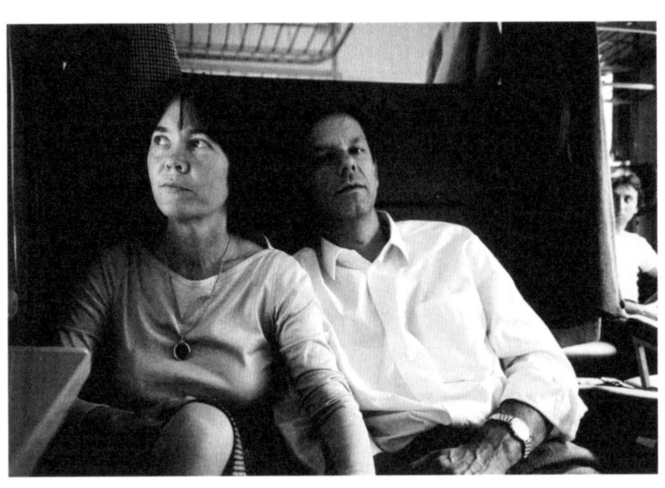

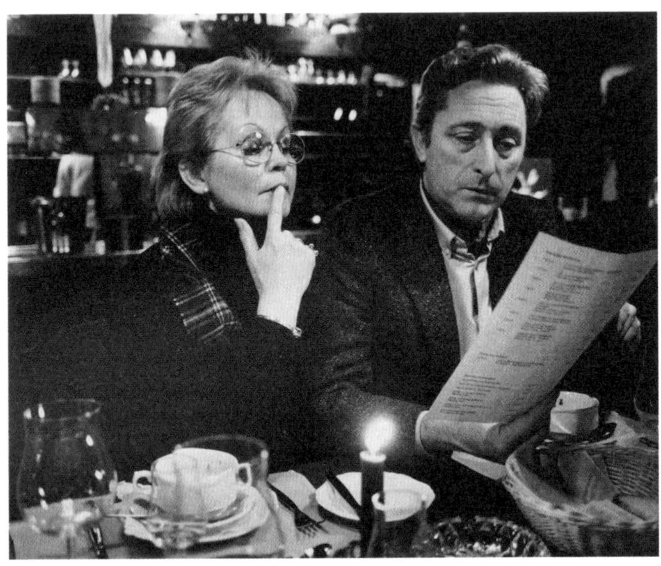

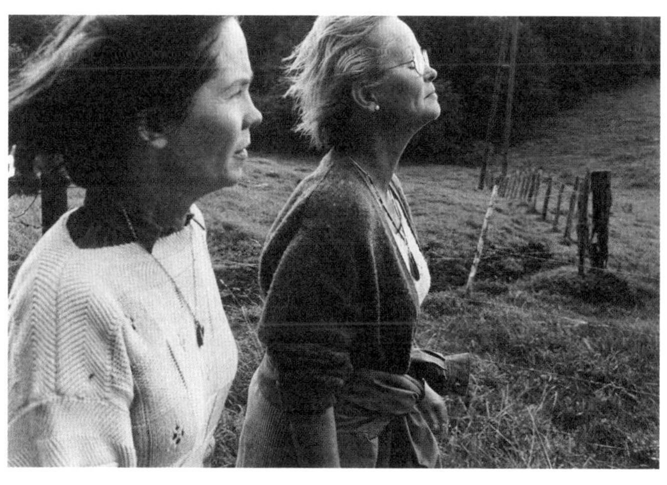

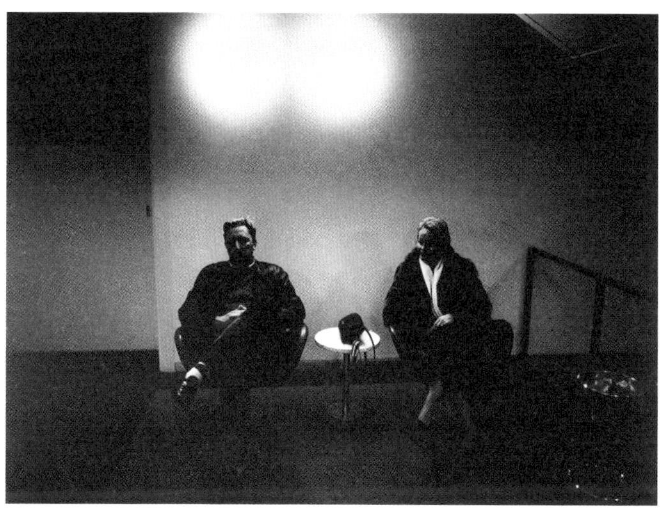

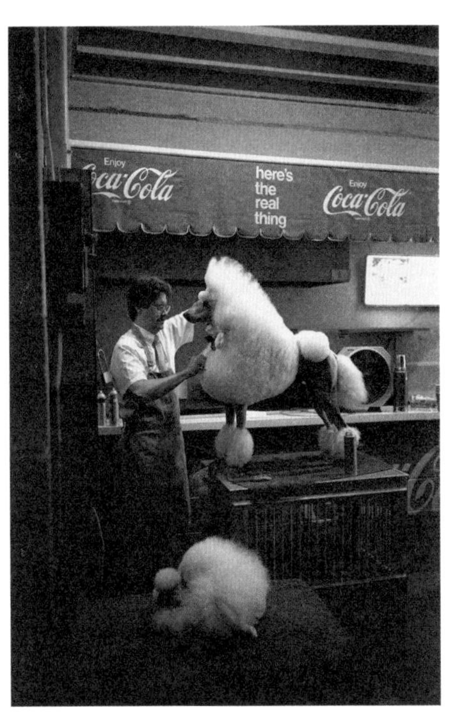
Enjoy
Coca-Cola
here's
the
real
thing
Enjoy
Coca-Cola

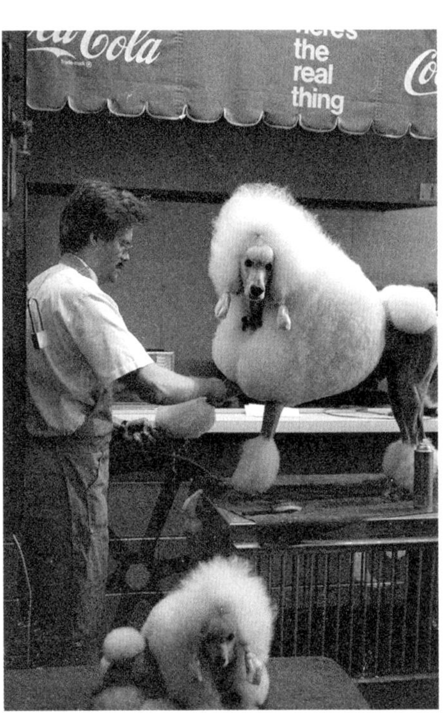
the
real
thing

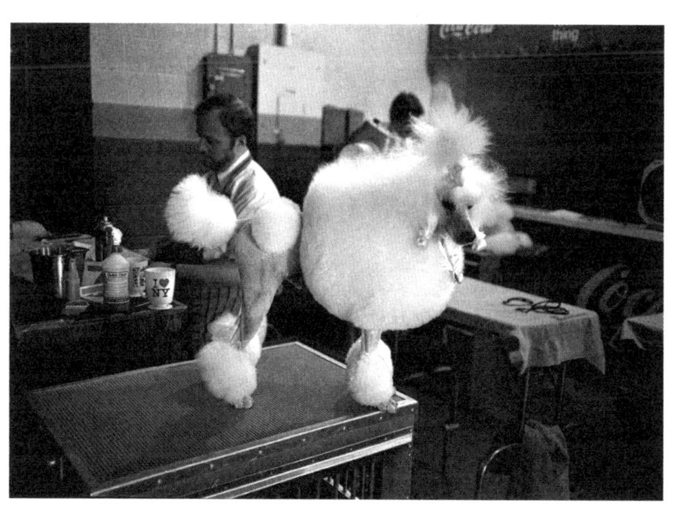
thing
I ♥ NY

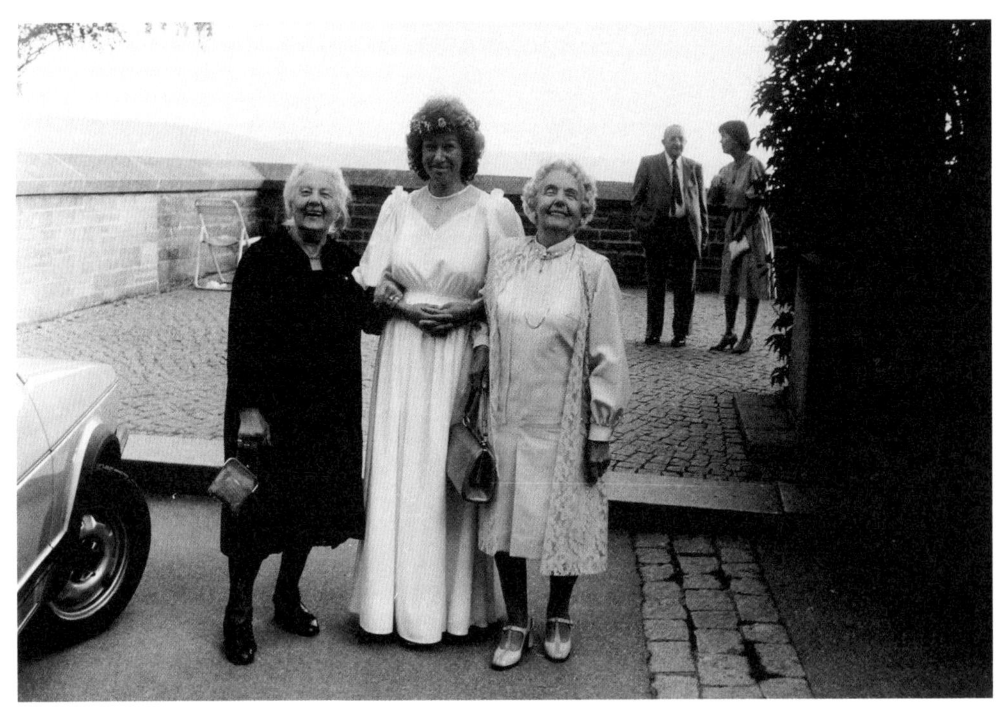

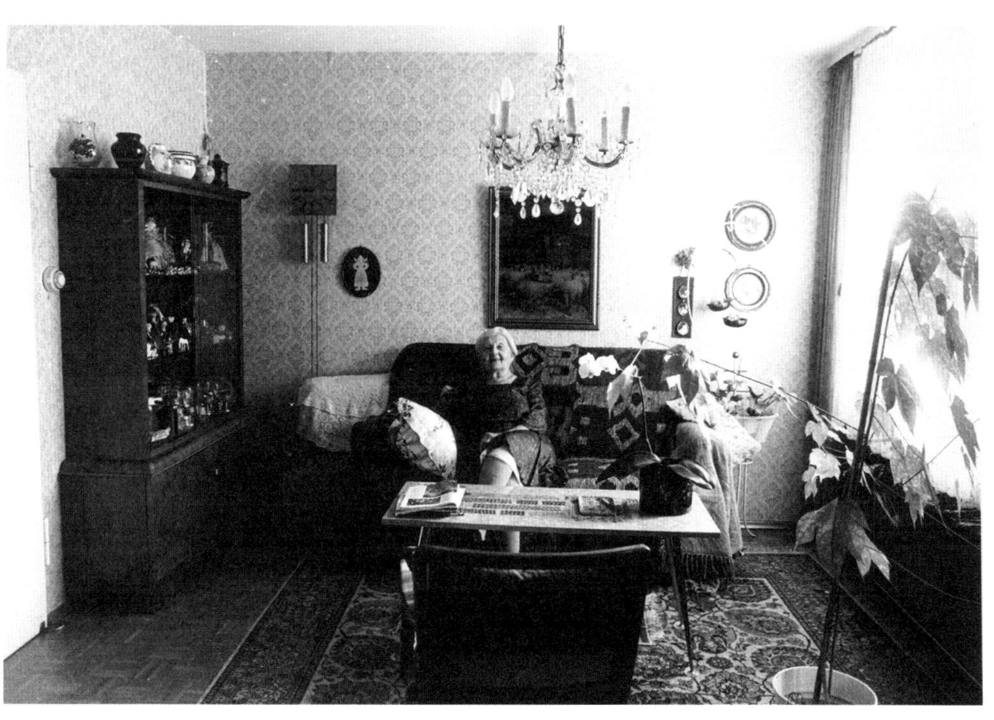

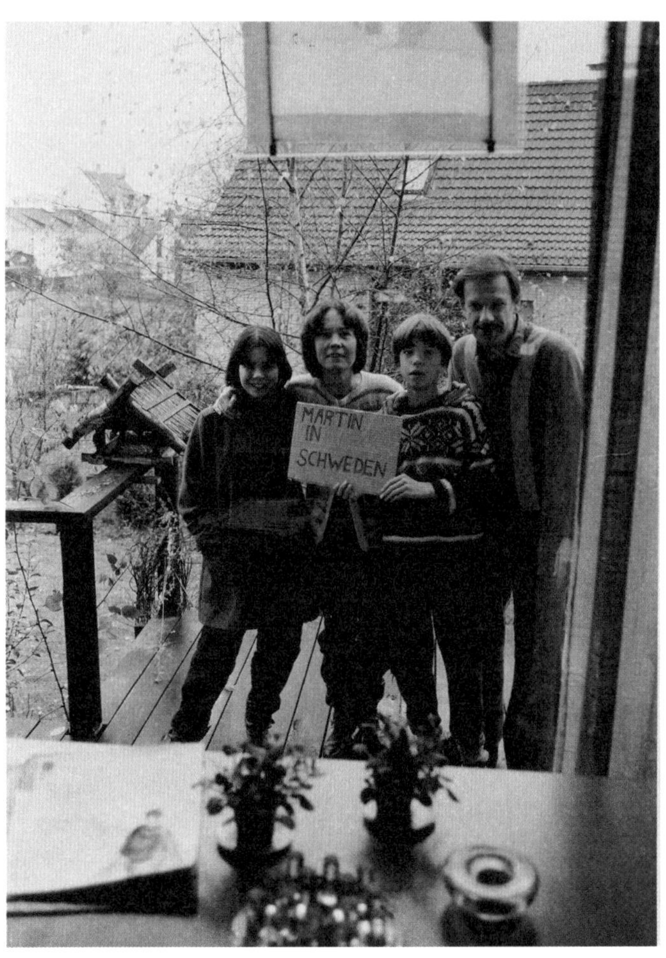
MARTIN
IN
SCHWEDEN

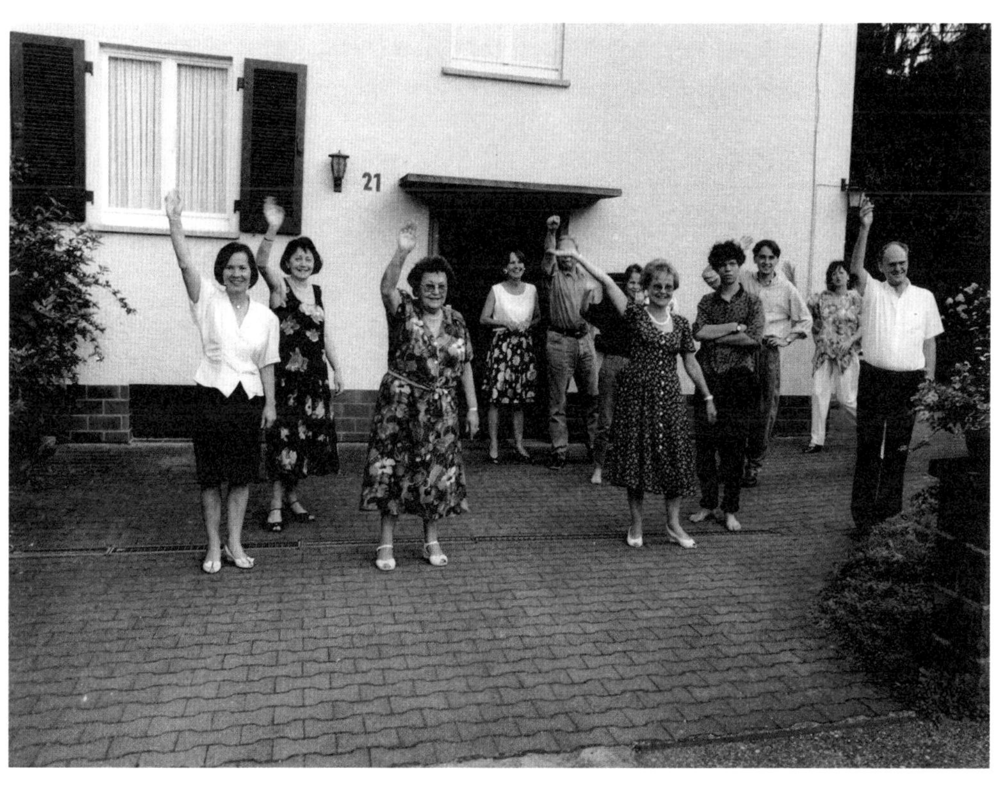
21

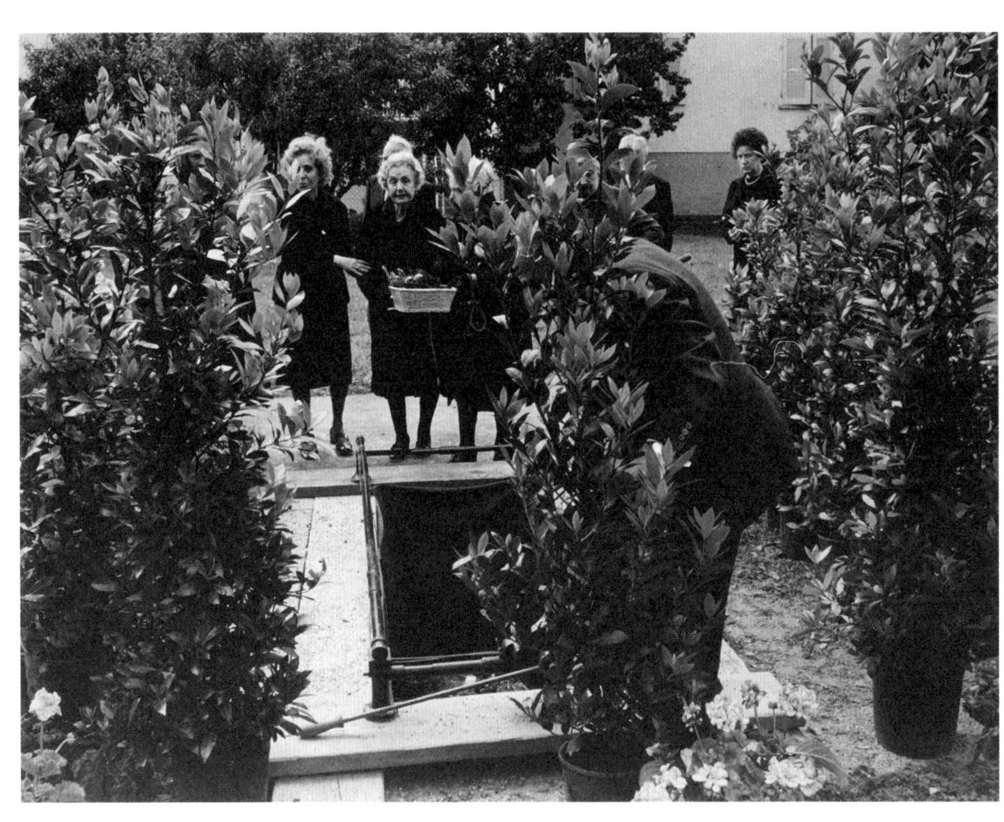

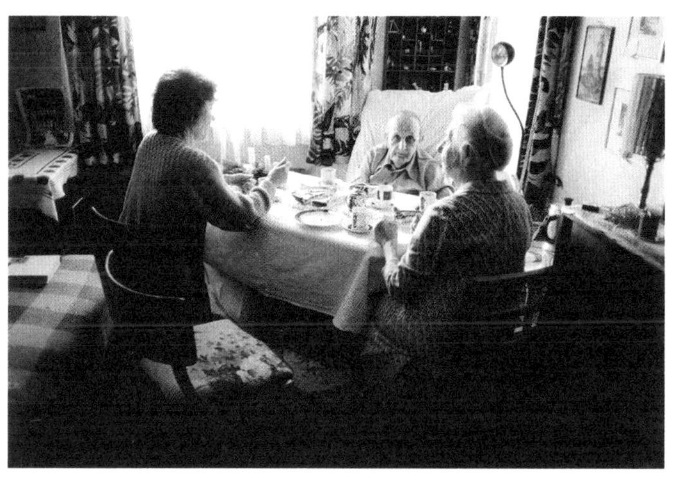

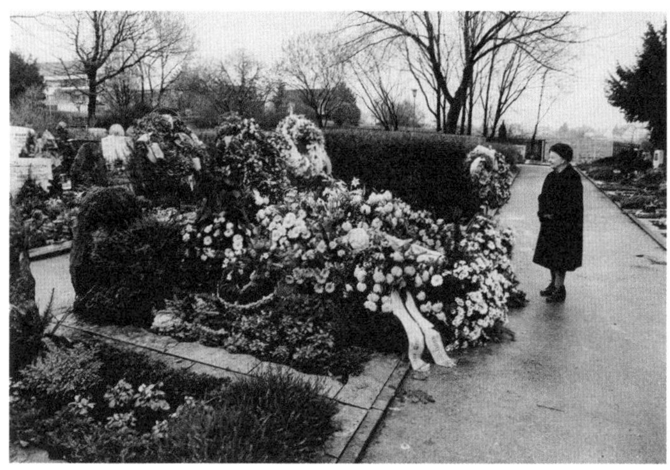

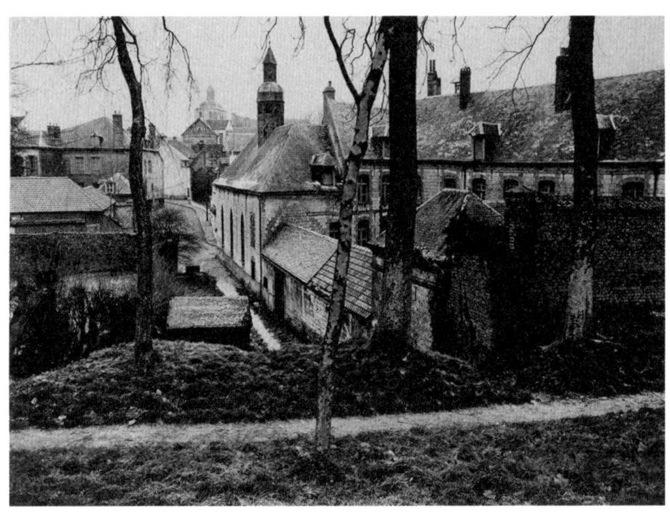

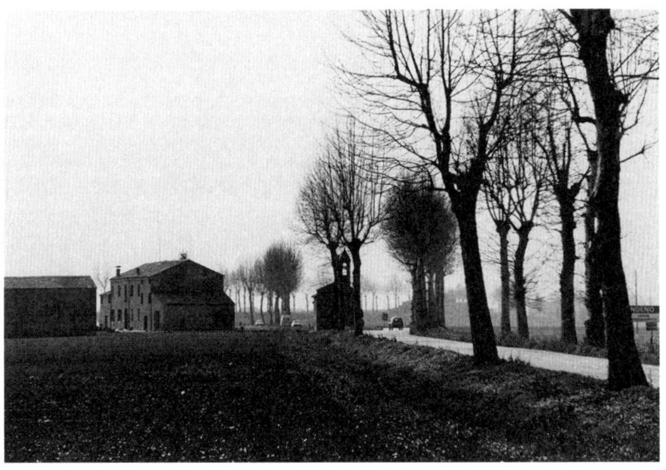

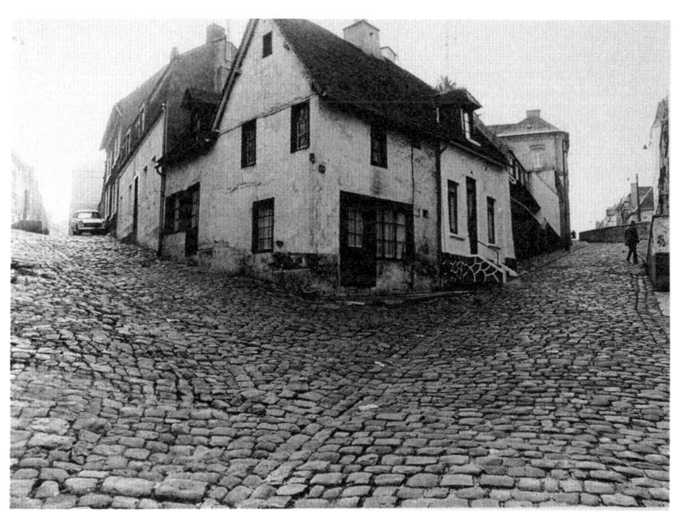

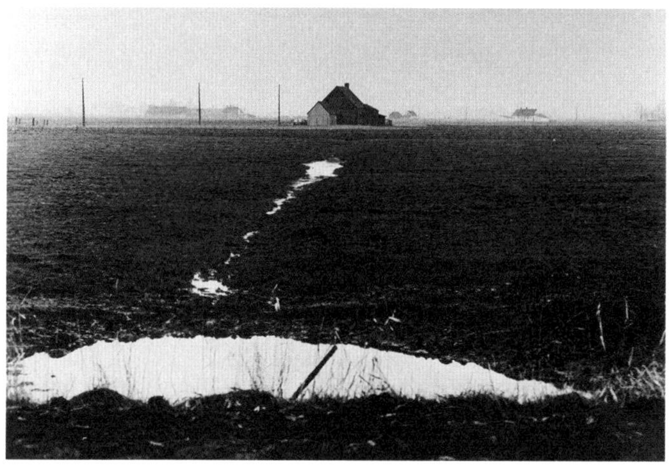

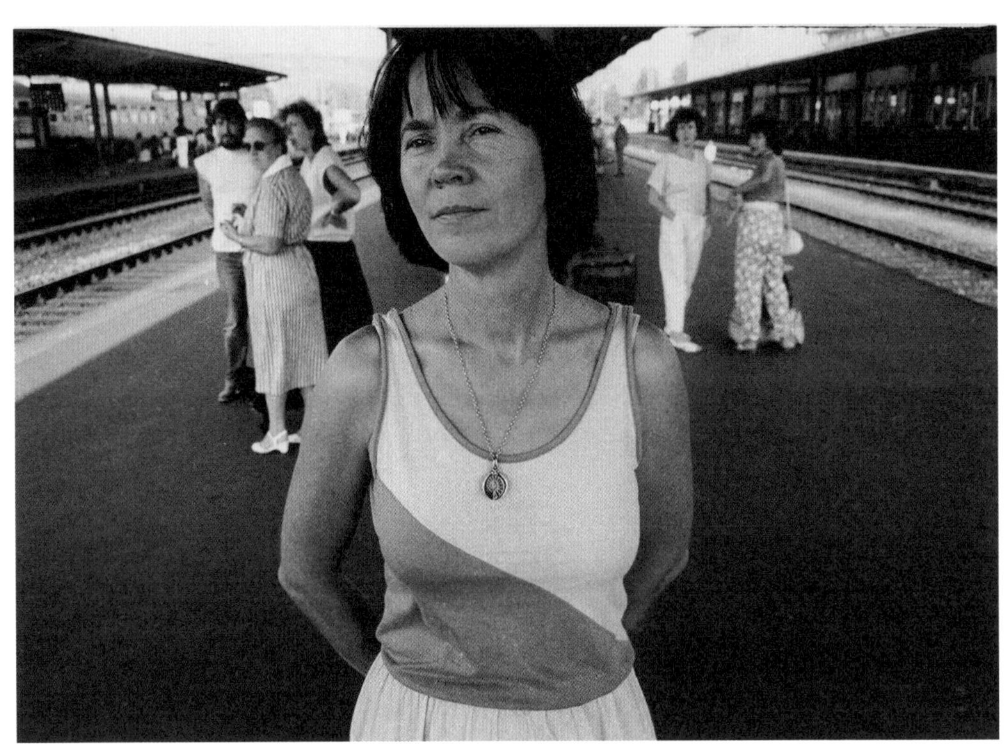

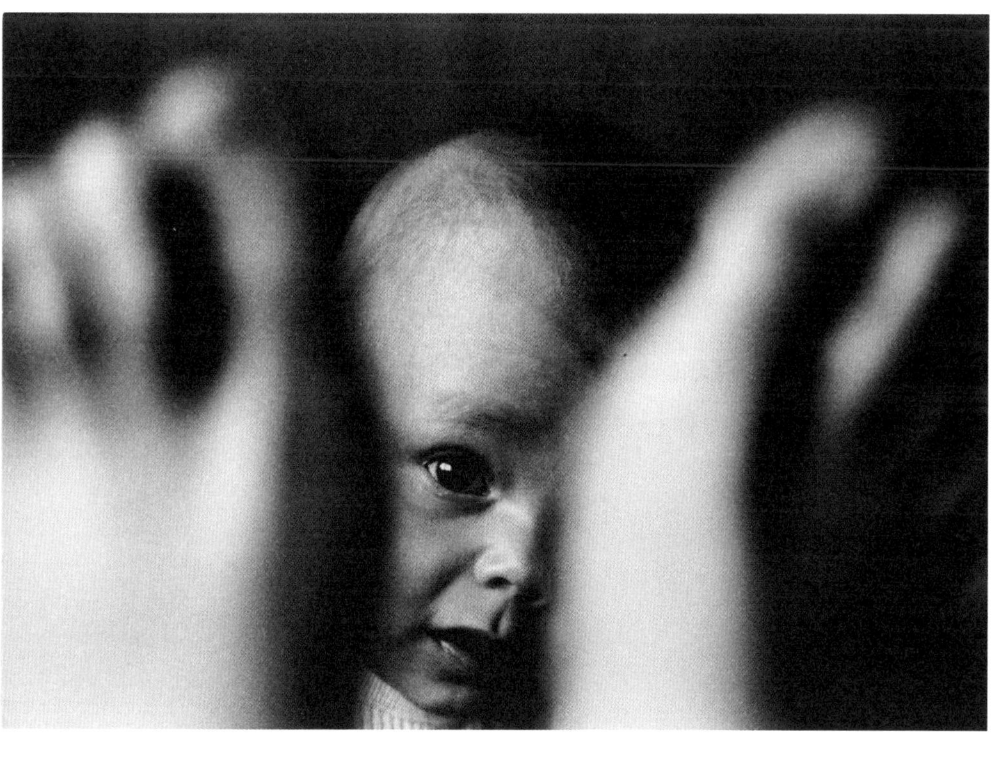

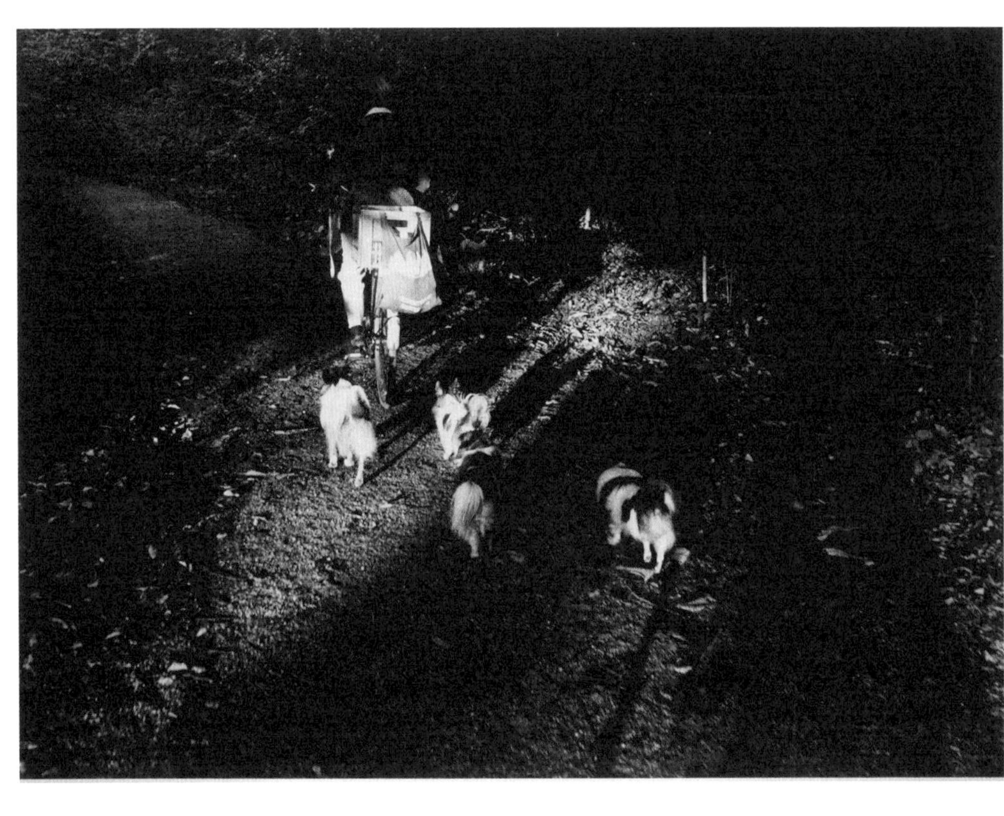

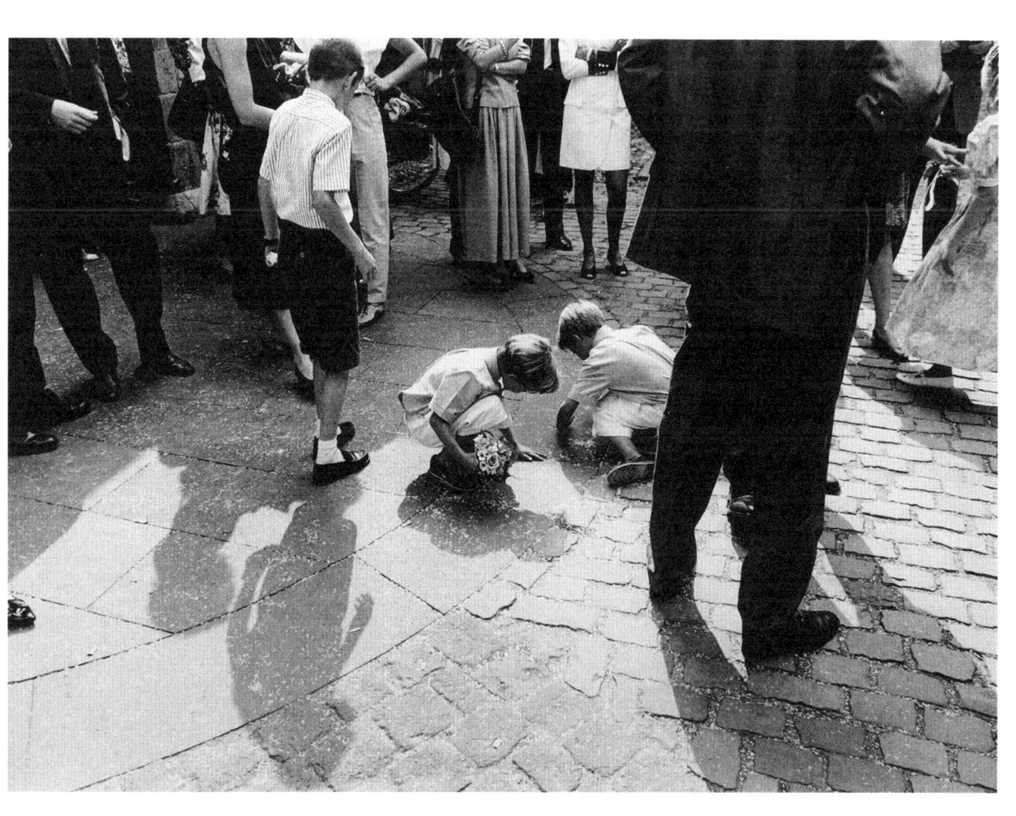

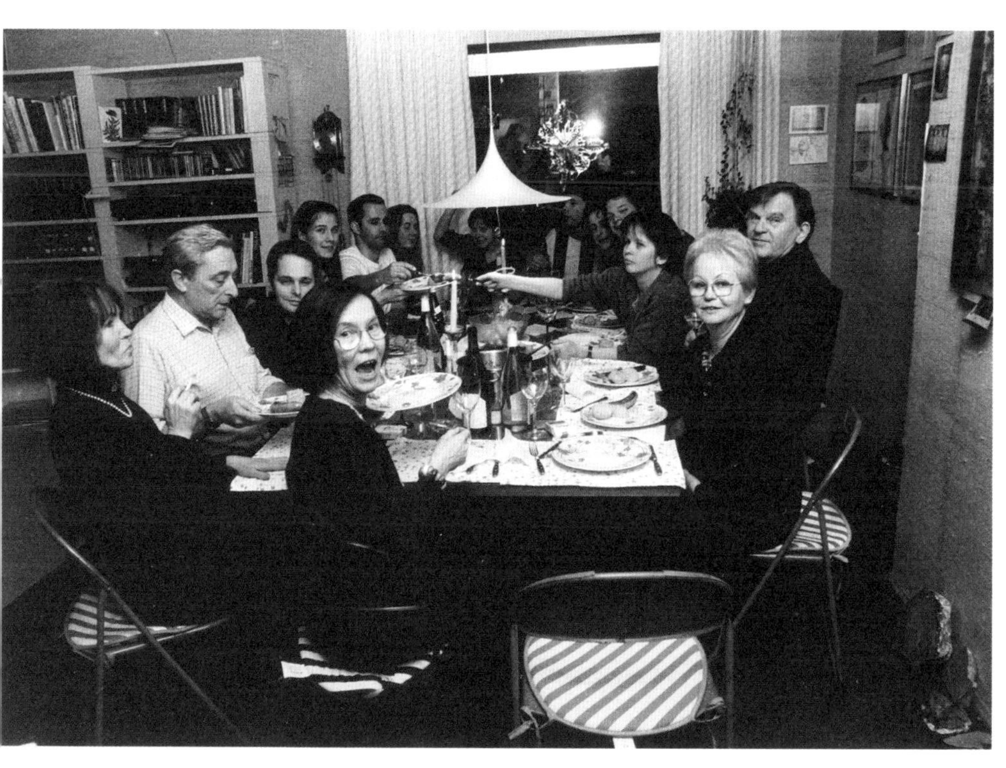

lost&found ist eine Buchreihe, in der verborgene oder verloren gegangene und wiederentdeckte Bildarchive vorgestellt werden. Sollten Sie ähnlich interessante Bilder kennen, melden Sie sich bei uns! Alle Bilder in dieser Publikation wurden nicht retuschiert.

lost&found is a book series that presents picture archives that were hidden or lost and have been rediscovered. If you are aware of similarly interesting pictures, please get in touch with us! All pictures in this publication are unretouched.

Die Publikation erscheint anlässlich der Ausstellung/This booklet is published in conjunction with the exhibition:

»Die reine Leidenschaft – Amateurfotografien von Peter Dammann, Eugen Gerbert, Axel Herrmann und Vasilii Lefter«, Opelvillen Rüsselsheim, 2. Mai – 29. Juli 2018 / May 2–July 29, 2018
www.opelvillen.de

Herausgegeben von/Edited by Beate Kemfert, Peter Dammann, Markus Hartmann

Lektorat und Übersetzung/Copyediting and translation:
Hans Georg Hiller von Gaertringen, Tas Skorupa
Gestaltung/Design: Antonia Größchen
Druck und Bindung: Druckerei Ziegler, Neckarbischofsheim
Produktion, Konzept, Verlag/Production, concept, publisher:
Hartmann Books, Rulfinger Straße 18, 70567 Stuttgart, Germany
www.hartmannprojects.com

Erste Auflage/First Edition: April 2018
Band/Volume: 3
ISBN 978-3-96070-024-1

Mit freundlicher Unterstützung von/
With generous support from

Stiftung Flughafen Frankfurt/Main
für die Region

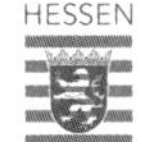

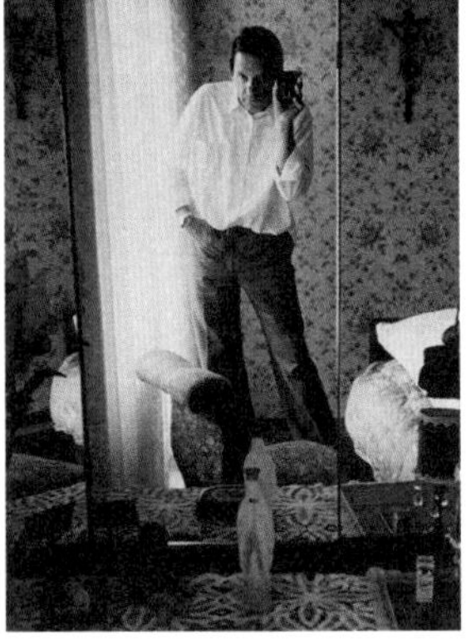